LANGUAGE ADVENTURES
WITH
Salt&Pepper
THE
BEST GIFTS
and Sunny

WRITTEN BY
JULIANA C. RUSSELL

ILLUSTRATED BY
MARCO ZERNERI

Let's learn Italian

molto
very

stanco
tired

svegliati
wake up

buongiorno!
good morning!

che facciamo?
what do we do?

che bello!
how nice!

vuoi
you want

voglio
I want

pasta fresca
freshly made pasta

compleanno
birthday

felice
happy

è vero!
that is true!

Scan me to learn italian!

LANGUAGE MINDSET

regalo
present

ciao!
hi!

a presto!
see you soon!

ti voglio bene!
I love you!

scoiattolo
squirrel

ho un'ottima idea!
I have a great idea!

gatto
cat

cuoco
cook

calcio
soccer

cane
dog

amica
friend

perfetto
perfect

andiamo
let's go

amici
friends

dai!
come on!

giochiamo!
let's play!

grazie di cuore
thank you very much

città
city

Salt and Pepper's very best friend is a squirrel, uno scoiattolo who lives in the tree nearby. Her name is Sunny.

I know the best regalo for our dear amica Sunny, lo scoiattolo!

What does Sunny want as a regalo?

What should Salt and Pepper get Sunny lo scoiattolo for her compleanno?

Salt is a gatto and an amazing cuoco he has a restaurant in town.

Pepper is a cane who loves to play calcio all over the world.

What does Sunny really love?

What would make her smile?

What would make her
molto felice?

"Amicizia e pasta sono meglio caldi."

"FRIENDSHIP AND PASTA ARE BEST WARM."

ITALIAN PROVERB

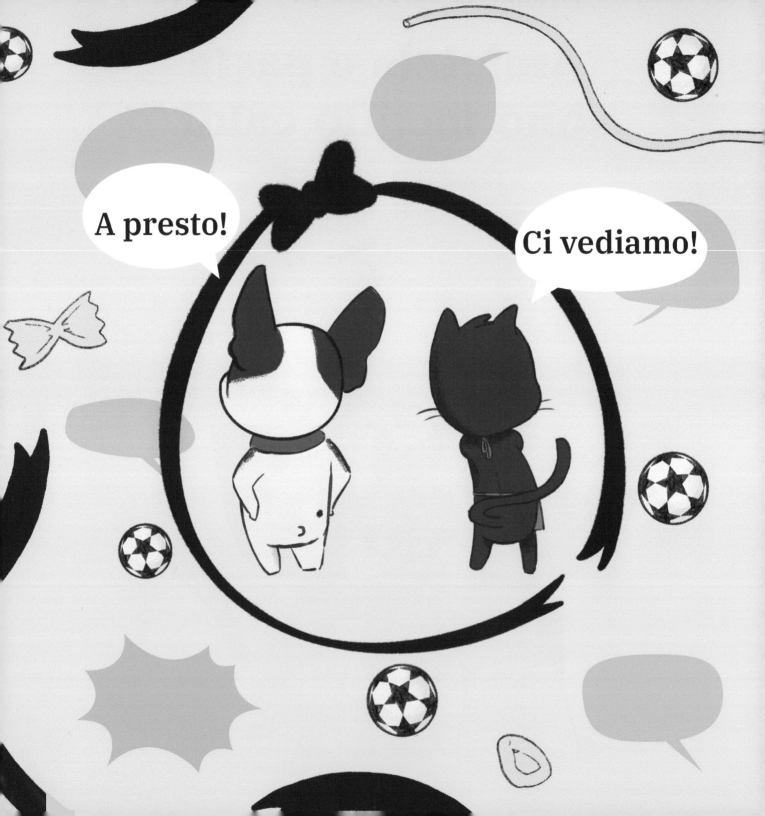

About the Author:

Grazie mille!

Juliana is a language enthusiast who is passionate about the transformative power of language. This love was ignited at the age of 15, failing a Spanish high-school class! After receiving a formal education in Spanish, Italian and French, she studied and lived in Spain, Italy, Argentina and traveled in France and Québéc. Through her immersion in different cultures, Juliana found the key to becoming proficient and excited about becoming multilingual. With that model in mind, she created her business, The Language Mindset, a school for children and adults.

When she isn't sharpening her linguistic skills, you can catch her snowboarding, horseback riding, reading books, and embroidery! She lives in upstate New York with her husband, cat, and dog.

Storytime is the most magical time to gather and enjoy a language learning journey. Are you ready for a language journey with Stories with Salt and Pepper?